CONTENTS

Page 1. Litter from the home front

3. Introduction

4. "Adolf in Blunderland"

6. "Look out in the black-out"

8. "Weigh your mummy's meat ration": food and clothes rationing

10. "Hitler will send no warning: remember your gas mask"

12. "BooBoo the Barrage Balloon"

13. "The Defence ABC"

14. "How to be safe from air raids"

16. "Put out your paper for salvage"

18. "Please save your cigarette and tobacco cartons"

20. "What to eat in wartime": recipes.

22. "Do your duty, send us greetings cards"

24. "Make do and mend"

26. "Make your jam with our help": magazines

28. "We want the Triumph": children's comics

30. "The Greatest Naval Game": the toy cupboard

32. "She's in love with a Soldier": song sheets

34. "Wings for Victory"

35. "ABC of aeroplane spotting"

36. "Dig for Victory"

38. "It's chocolate, it's food": sweets

40. "Lend a hand on the land"

42. "Our Wonderful Women"

44. "Back up the fighting forces"

46. "Laugh it off"

48. "Who wants blinking Search lights tonight?": comic postcards

50. "The best buy for the wise G.I."

51. ENSA Munition Concerts

52. "Keep the flag flying!"

54. "Food needs transport — don't waste it": kitchen cupboard

56. "VE Day — it's all over!"

58. "Careless talk costs lives": the war of the words

59. A space for your family memories

60. "Beat the Blitz" game: have fun playing this.

Signs of the times: the traditional china teapot replaced the aluminium one; the novelty toilet roll poured derision on the Nazis — "S(h)it down with Goering" and "Use Hess paper for Mess paper".

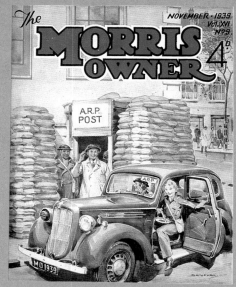

Mistaken Identity
Home Guard (defending force)
"Bang! Bang! You're dead."

Soldier (attacking force):
"Chug! Chug! I'm a tank."

Where did Mr Chad (later
Mr Watno) come from?
Nobody seems to know.

A week's ration mid-war:
2oz of tea, 8oz of sugar, 4oz of jam,
3oz of sweets, 2oz of lard, 2oz of butter,
2oz of margarine, 4oz of cheese,
4oz of bacon, 3/4 lb of meat, one egg
(sometimes).

INTRODUCTION

As the sandbags were piled high, barrage balloons
released in the sky, and the children evacuated,
Britain made ready for battle on the home front –
gas masks, blackouts, air raids, rationing, shortages
and queues. The posters of propaganda, information
and encouragement went up, the leaflets of survival
were distributed, and the nation was transformed into
a culture where each was "doing their bit", because
"we're all in it together". Every component of daily life
took on the mantle of war – bus tickets and milk
bottle tops bore slogans like "raw material is war
material" and "milk for vigour and victory".

Products adapted quickly to the new situation; the word game
of Lexicon was promoted as providing "hours of fun and
entertainment during the blackout nights", while Puritan
soap gave "double ration lather"; the cereal Bemax in a
tin made it "gas-proof", and Frys Chocolate Spread "solves
the butter problem". Ingenuity eked out precious supplies:
"Teafusa gets more out of your tea", and Rynchene
saved clothing coupons by "making old garments
look and feel like new". Endless new
games were devised, such as "Rafies
Rollicking Trip to Berlin" (an
adaptation of the Silver Bullet
puzzle of the First World War).
Even the paper bags into which the
products went sported slogans, like
"food is a munition of war, don't waste it".

Humour constantly welled up, even in the worst
circumstances. Bombed shopkeepers joked,
"More open than usual", "Bismuth as usual" (chemist),
and on a barber's shop next to a blitzed building,
"We've had a close shave. Come and get one yourself."
Radio shows like ITMA ("It's That Man Again") and
"Hi, Gang!" kept up the spirits of the whole nation.
The radio was also the focal point for popular music as
well as the more serious side of life from news
bulletins to the Radio Doctor.

Since 1940 the Victory Waltz had been played by
Joe Loss and "For Victory" painting books coloured
in, but when victory finally came souvenirs were
limited, the most adventurous being a winding
panorama of the Victory parade.

This is a scrapbook of daily life during the
Second World War. It is a celebration of those
difficult yet inspiring years when ordinary
people showed such extraordinary powers of
good humour and steadfastness.

"Gift Lists. Owing to war
conditions always write
for an up-to-date gift
list before sending coupons."

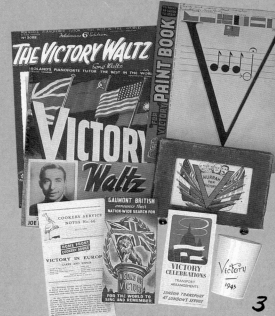

3

Lampooned by cartoonists, Hitler and his cronies were made fun of at every opportunity. Jokes were often lavatorial and well-known books were parodied, becoming popular sellers ("Adolf in Blunderland" had reached its fourth edition three months after publication in December 1939). Funds from the sales of "Struwwelhitler", a parody on the original "Struwwelpeter", went to the Daily Sketch War Relief Fund which supplied woollen comforts to the services and food to air raid victims.

4

"Yes, Dear, we got on all right in the Black-out, but he had to put three layers of tissue-paper over his torch!"

Safety in the Black-out !

A LITTLE ♥ YOU CAN'T BLACK-OUT !

SOMEWHERE IN THE BLACK-OUT !

? **Why Risk Your Life**

THEATRE IN BLACK-OUT

THE PLAYHOUSES are emerging from darkness—em... surely. We wait in our own private darknesses and... resurrection. They are indispensable at all times, in p...

that... ...re than Ar... ...guard the...

histo... ...prints, th...
and... Siddons...
Irvin... ...e "made...

...THEATR...
...for all v...
...CHE...
...LONDON...

"Oh, Girls, I've been kissed in the black-out!"

A BLACK-OUT'S A BLACK-OUT AND SHE MUST BE TOLD—TO-MORROW.

"PUT THAT BLINKIN' LIGHT OUT!"

"Not A Black-Out-Look!"

BLACK-OUT!

I'D LIKE TO BE NEAR YOU IN THE BLACK-OUT.

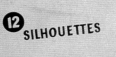

12 SILHOUETTES

A FRIENDLY ARGUMENT 12

12 YOUR LIGHT'S SHOWING

11 SILHOUETTES

AIR-RAID WARDEN 11

The Amusing Topical Card Game

BLACK-OUT!

The Game to cheer you up

EVERYBODY'S PLAYING IT!

YOUR LIGHT'S SHOWING

BLACK-OUT FASHIONS

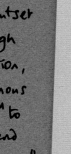

KATIE'S COSTUME 01

LOOK OUT IN THE BLACK-OUT

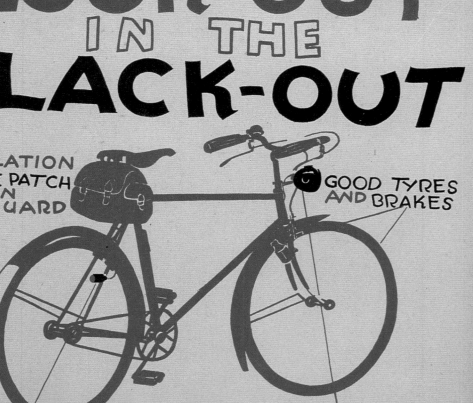

REGULATION WHITE PATCH ON MUDGUARD

GOOD TYRES AND BRAKES

Black-outs were enforced from the outset of war and regrettably caused a huge increase in road accidents. One solution, though ineffective, was to wear luminous badges or Mack's Luminous Armlets "to avoid being knocked down by cars and cyclists or bumped into by other pedestrians."

8D

Coupon Savers

BLOUSES, SKIRTS
JACKETS, BOLEROS, ETC.

TWO-WAY
BOLERO
& FOUR-WAY
SKIRT
PATTERN

These Blouse Patterns

No. 273

SEPTEMBER 6, 1941

Woman

THREEPENCE

COMPLETE STORY
by Lyn Arnold

NEW EMBROIDERY
in Full Colour

AUTUMN FROCK
in Five Styles

HOW TO CHOOSE YOUR FOOD

Your Ration Book

Issued to ...

WELDON
FASHION SERIES No. 487

Practical Wear

for WAR WORK

6D

FREE *inside*
PATTERN of smart
SHIRT and OVERALL

This book is the property of His Majesty's Government.

MOTOR SPIRIT RATION BOOK No.

For the months of AUGUST, SEPTEMBER and OCTOBER, 1940

AF 31839

M/C
NOT EXCEEDING
250 c.c.

Motor Cycle
(including Auto-cycle)

Registered Number of Vehicle
ECV 889

Date and Office of Issue

LISKEARD
22 JLY 40
CORNWALL

The coupons in this book authorise the furnishing
and acquisition of the number of units of motor
spirit specified on the coupons subject to the
conditions appearing thereon.

ANY PERSON FURNISHING OR ACQUIRING
WITH THE CONDITIONS ON WHICH
TO PROSECUTION.

The issue of a Ration Book does not guarantee to
the holder any minimum quantity of motor spirit
and the book may be cancelled at any time within

CLOTHING COUPON

QUIZ

2nd Edition Revised

Answers to Questions
on the Rationing of
Clothing, Footwear, Cloth
and Knitting Yarn

Crown Copyright reserved

MINISTRY OF FOOD

PAGE 1

RATION BOOK
SUPPLEMENT

This is a Spare Book

YOU WILL BE TOLD
HOW AND WHEN TO USE IT

HOLDER'S NAME AND REGISTERED ADDRESS

Surname   GIBBS

Other Names   Mabel

Address   Marshfort
                 Hailsham

If found, please return to
HAILSHAM, S.E. 33.

NATIONAL REGISTRATION NO.

ERNI 9 1

FOOD OFFICE

OFFICIAL
PAID

1942-43 CLOTHING BOOK

This book may not be used until the holder's name, full postal
address and National Registration (Identity Card) Number
have been plainly written below in INK.

NAME   RUTENBERG DANIEL
(BLOCK LETTERS)

ADDRESS   2 GROSVENOR GARDENS
(BLOCK LETTERS)

(TOWN)   LONDON SW1 (COUNTY)

NATIONAL REGISTRATION (IDENTITY CARD) NUMBER

AKBU   192   3 X

Read the instructions within carefully, and take great care not to lose this book.

Food rationing began
in January 1940 - during one
of the coldest winters on record.
To cut out the ration coupons,
some grocers used specially
adapted scissors which cut
round the corners. Children
could buy their own weighing
scales and dolly's ration book.

Clothing was rationed from June '41.

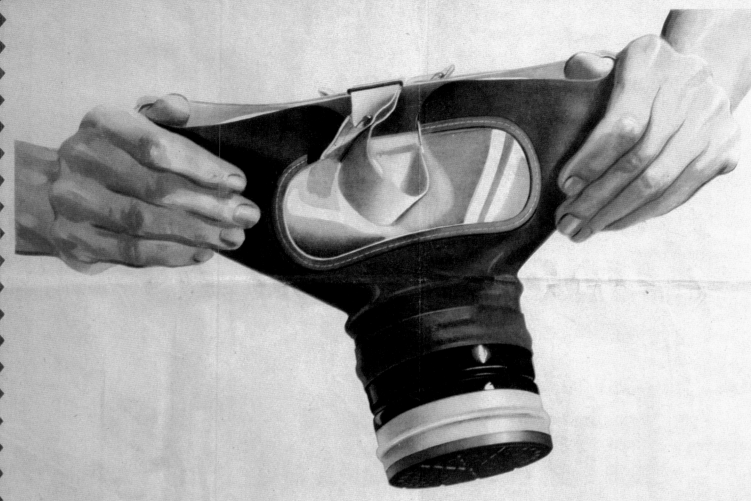

Hitler will send no warning –

so always carry your gas mask

ISSUED BY THE MINISTRY OF HOME SECURITY

10

A touch of humour made the fearful gas mask more endurable. For children a look-a-like Mickey Mouse mask was more fun (it was later withdrawn as it used too many scarce resources). Ladies found that the obligatory gas mask box doubled up as a handbag to carry face powder and other essentials.

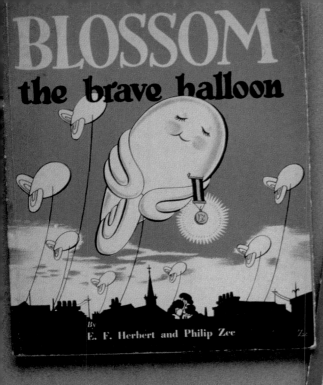

BLOSSOM the brave balloon
By E. F. Herbert and Philip Zec

by **Enid Marx**
BULGY *the Barrage Balloon*

A Balloon
of One's Own
St John Cooper

Boo-Boo
THE BARRAGE BALLOON

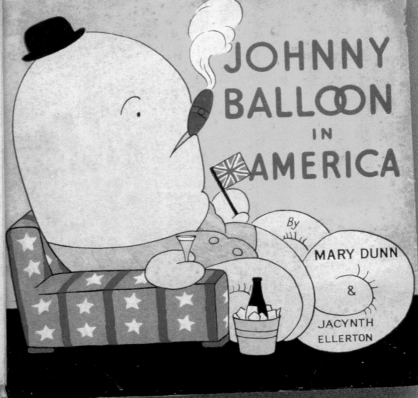

JOHNNY BALLOON IN AMERICA
By MARY DUNN & JACYNTH ELLERTON

At night, too, he was always on guard, and he often had jolly talks with the man in the moon and some of the saucy cats that climbed on to the roof tops for a chinwag.

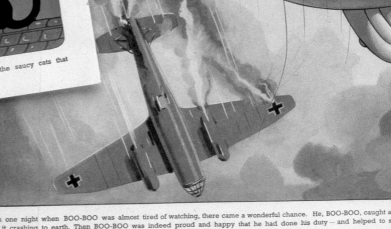

Then one night when BOO-BOO was almost tired of watching, there came a wonderful chance. He, BOO-BOO, caught an enemy aeroplane and sent it crashing to earth. Then BOO-BOO was indeed proud and happy that he had done his duty — and helped to save the land he loved.

A common sight over British cities during the war was the barrage balloon. Converted by the story teller, they became friendly characters in children's books. One adventure has 'Boo-Boo' ensnaring an enemy aeroplane in its holding wire.

12

A —STANDS FOR "A.B.[...]" A FIRST-CLASS SAILO[...]

E —STANDS FOR EVACS. OF VARIOUS SIZES WHO FIND COUNTRY LIFE BRIMFUL OF SURPRISES

K —IS FOR KIT YOU SEE WHAT A MESS IT IS WHO MINDS A BIT—IT'S ALL BARE NECESSITIES

F —STANDS FOR FRENCHMAN THE POILU POLITE A GAY LITTLE FELLOW BUT A DEMON TO FIGH[...]

L —IS FOR LANCERS WHERE MEN OF ALL RANKS HAVE GIVEN UP HORSES AND TAKEN TO TANKS

Q —IS THE QUEUES SEEN EVERYWHERE OF THOSE WHO ARE WAITING TO SHOULDER THEIR SHARE

U —ARE THE U BOATS WHO ALWAYS ATTACK A SHIP WHEN THEY KNOW THAT IT CANNOT HIT BACK

THE DEFENCE ABC

PAINTING BOOK

By Hassall

R —FOR REFUGEES FROM VARIO[...] WHO COME HERE TO LIVE [...]

[...] THE VETS AS STABLE AS WHEN [...] WERE CAMELS & HORSES ENGAGED WITH THE MEN

C —COMES FROM CANAD[...] AS HARD AS THEY MA[...]

D —IS FOR DUG-OUT WHERE GRANDPAPA READS WHILE GRANDMAMA KNITS THE SOCKS THAT HE NEEDS

N —IS THE NAVY WHOSE POWER IS IMMENSE OUR PRIDE & OUR GLORY OUR SHIELD & DEFENCE

A John Hassall masterpiece produced at the outbreak of war.

'A' was also for "Airman already to fly with millions of pamphlets to drop from the sky."

Daily Mail

FOR KING AND EMPIRE

NO. 13,941

ONE PENNY

LATE WAR NEWS SPECIAL

Cycle Accessories
LIGHTWEIGHT FEATHERWEIGHT NOWEIGHT
Bluemel's

Hitler Planned Monday Swoop

London was to Blaze First

By NOEL MONKS,
Daily Mail Air Correspondent

HITLER meant to start the second Great Fire of London as the prelude to an invasion.

WAR'S GREATEST PICTURE: St. Paul's Stands Unharmed in the Midst of the Burning City

America Moves

BIG ARMS FLOW HAS BEGUN

From Daily Mail Correspondent
NEW YORK, Monday.

THE United States Defence Commission announced to-day that they had approved arms contracts worth £2,500,000,000.

Monthly production had now risen to 2,400 aircraft engines, 700 warplanes, 100 tanks, and 10,000 automatic rifles.

Present British and American orders on hand total 50,000 planes, 130,000 aero-engines, 9,200 tanks, 2,955,000 guns, 390 naval vessels, 200 merchant ships, 50,000 lorries, and other equipment.

The United States Government were building 40 war factories, including the first plant for mass-producing tanks.

* Hitler Will Reply to Roosevelt—Page FIVE.

LATEST

MAN, WIFE DEAD IN W.1 FLAT

Yard early to-day were investigating mysterious death of a man and his wife, aged about 50, in luxury flat, at Bickenhall Mansions, Baker-street, W.1. No signs to indicate the causes of death. Sir Bernard Spilsbury may be called in to make a post-mortem.

FIRE OVER LONDON

The Story of The London Fire Service 1940-41
ONE SHILLING

WE ARE ON THE JOB..

BOMBERS OVER LONDON
by TED BRAMLEY
Price 1d.

SONG in the SHELTER

By BERNARD HENRY 4D.

THE BATTLE OF BRITAIN

A.R.P.
THE PRACTICAL AIR RAID PROTECTION BRITAIN NEEDS
1D.

How much protection will the Government's air raid precautions give? What is being done against high explosive bombs? Can the refuge room be a real refuge? Is the British public being fooled?

Endless pamphlets, booklets and leaflets were issued to ensure everyone could take protective measures against the devastation of bombing — sandbags, shelters, anti-shatter lacquer.

COMPLETE AIR RAID PRECAUTION

A·B·C of A·R·P 6D
ILLUSTRATING HOME OFFICE INSTRUCTIONS
SECOND (Revised and Enlarged) EDITION

A PICTURE GUIDE
for Householders & A.R.P. Personnel

CONTENTS include—
- Air Raid Warnings
- Construction of Shelters and Trenches
- Notes on High Explosive
- Precautions Against Incendiary Bombs
- Poison Gas Tables
- All about Gas Masks and Babies' Helmets
- Gas-proof Clothing and Decontamination
- Pets and Animals
- Evacuation

INCENDIARY BOMBS

EXPLOSIVES

ANDERSON SHELTER
...CE SHELTER

AIR-RAID PRECAUTION
INDIA HOUSE.
EMERGENCY INSTRUCTIO...
Room No. 403
Indication of an impending Air Raid given by the sounding of a Typhon Horn.
On...

A.R.P.
HOME STORAGE OF FOOD SUPPL...
What to buy and how to use

MINISTRY OF HOME SECURITY
1940
Air Raids

HOW TO BE SAFE FROM AIR...
62 PAGES 2D
BY PROFESSOR...

"I'VE JUST BEEN SHOWING MISS JONES OUR AIR RAID SHELTER, DARLING!"

Lilliput
...OBER VOL.9. N° 4...
1/-

A Series of Charts giving full instructions as to Air Raid Precautions, Gas Effects and Recognition and Treatment of Injuries

ESSENTIAL TO FIRE WATCHERS

AIR RAID FIRST AID
Eighth Impres...
AUTHORITATIVE CLEAR CONCISE

A·R·P
AIR RAID WARDEN

WARDEN'S REPORT FORM.
Form of Report to Report Centres.
(Commence with the words) "AIR RAID DAMAGE"
Designation of REPORTING AGENT (e.g., Warden's Sector Number)

A.R.P.
Shatter-Resisting Mixture
The perfect window protection against bomb blast and shrapnel splin...ters. Absolutely transparent and defin...tely prevents glass splinters.
Will res...d cold and can be washed...

WAR TIME FIRST AID for EVERYMAN
E. G. BAILEY

EMERGOPLAST FLEXIBLE FIRST AID WOUND DRESSINGS
READY FOR IMMEDIATE APPLICATION
Boots
TO BE STORED IN A COOL PLACE

70 FT. LONG 2 INS. WIDE
SPECIALLY PREPARED
AIR RAID PRECAUTION
SEALING TAPE
6D EACH

ABSORBENT Cotton Wool
FINE QUALITY, B.P.C.
Medical and Surgical Requisites
Sold at...

THE HOUSEHOLDERS' FIRST AID CASE for A.R.P.
CONTENTS:
BURN DRESSINGS, medium
ADHESIVE PLASTER
...OOL (FOR PADDING OR DRESSING)
EMERGOPLAST WOUND DRESSINGS
...CTURE OF IODINE ½ oz.
...ETY PINS
AT ALL BRANCHES
BOOTS PURE DRUG CO. LTD.

A·R·P
...R LONDONERS
WHITE OPEN-WOVE BANDAGE
1 in. by 3 yds.

SURGEON'S ZINC OXIDE ADHESIVE PLASTER
ADHERES WITHOUT HEAT OR MOISTURE
IMPROVED ANTISEPTIC

ZINC OXIDE ADHESIVE...

BURNOL ACRIFLAVINE CREAM
THE BEST FIRST-AID TREATMENT FOR ALL KINDS OF WOUNDS, ABRASIONS AND BURNS
PREPARED BY Boots

ANTI-SHATTER LACQUER "CLEEROL"
...gives best protection against flying glass splinters in air raids.
...gives a perfectly clear and transparent film which does not restrict light.
...resistant to weather, can be washed with water and is easily removed when re...quired...
LUPSO LTD. 109 KINGSWAY LONDON

EMERGENCY WOUND BANDETTES DRESSINGS

SPECIALLY PREPARED
AIR RAID PRECAUTIONS /...
GLASS RE-INFORCING KRAFT PA...

WHITE OPEN-WOVE...

Packings for Cereals, Sugar, Dried Egg, Flour, Cigarettes, Cleaning Powder, *appear by kind permission of* **Mrs. Housewife** *whose paper salvage made the cartons*

REGINALD MOUNT

PUT OUT YOUR PAPER FOR SALVAGE

ISSUED BY THE BOARD OF TRADE. B.O.T. 224   PRINTED FOR H.M. STATIONERY OFFICE BY NORBURY, LOCKWOOD & CO. LTD., CHEETHAM, MANCHESTER, 8. 51-2817

STILL M...

PAPER RAGS BONES
WANTED FOR SALVAGE

WASTE PAPER

including wra... paper, cardb... cardboard ... letters, e... books, ne...

Tie the...

YOUR "EMPTIES" WANTED

Please bring back your empty cod liver oil and orange juice bottles when you com... for a new supply

MINISTRY OF F...

WANTED URGENTLY

MAKE SURE OF YOUR JAM RATION BY RETURNING EVERY EMPTY **NOW**

EMPTY JAM JARS

Please return a jar for each full one bought

WARNING!

Any person **BURNING OR DESTROYING WASTEPAPER**

(WRAPPING PAPER, CARDBOARD BOXES, ENVELOPES, NEWSPAPERS, MAGAZINES, ETC.)

IS GUILTY OF AN OFFENCE AGAINST THE NATIONAL WAR EFFORT

Every scrap is needed for essential national requirements.

Save it for local Council collections.

if **THEY** starve

WE starve

SAVE YOUR SCRAPS OF FOOD!

Mrs Smith is helping to win the war.

Cod Liver Oil compound

CONCENTRATED ORANGE JUICE

Request to the Retailers

Will you save this Box when empty with other Yardley packing material until you have an economical quantity for return. Please also encourage your customers to return their empty Boxes to you. A generous allowance will be paid you in National Savings Stamps.

SCARCITY OF BOTTLES

PLEASE RETURN ALL EMPTIES NEXT ROUND

With the shortage of raw materials, everyone was encouraged to return bottles, tins and paper, even food scraps. On the leaflet (right), a pencilled message says, "The councils roadsweeper will collect kitchen waste if put outside Tuesday and friday 8am."

BLACKCURRANT JAM ROWNTREE & CO. LTD. YORK

CHIVERS Strawberry Jam

Armitage's BLACKBERRY & APPLE

Nelson STRAWBERRY

TINS ARE SHORT...

OWING TO WAR CONDITIONS

Please put your Jugs out on Monday morning February 15th.

Cigarettes and tobacco were considered morale-boosters during the war and although restricted, continued to be available (queues quickly formed to a shop delivery). Cigarette cards ceased at the outbreak of war and advertising showcards stopped being made in 1940 to save paper. As the war progressed, card packets were used less and replaced by paper wrappers; less ink was used and designs were modified accordingly. Tobacco tins carried a request for their return to the tobacconist.

GREEN VEGETABLES

No country in the world grows vegetables better than we do, and probably no country in the world cooks them worse. For generations we have wasted our root vegetables by excessive peeling and over-cooking, and boiled most of the goodness out of our green vegetables—only to pour it down the sink.

When fresh fruit is short we need green vegetables more than ever because they all contain the important fresh fruit vitamin, Vitamin C. Some have more than others. Brussels Sprouts, parsley and watercress all contain more than oranges; cabbage, cauliflower, spinach, swede, broccoli, turnip tops and kale are all good sources of this vitamin. Not only do green vegetables give us vitamin C, but also vitamins A and B, iron and calcium. Green peas and beans, bread, French and runner, make a welcome change in the summer months, but remember they do not take the place of the leafy, green vegetables, as they contain only a little vitamin C. See that you have a salad a day as well as peas and beans when they are in season.

MINISTRY OF FOOD LEAFLET No. 1

IRENE VEAL suggests some war-time CAKES

Some of these recipes were entries in the RADIO TIMES WARTIME CAKE COMPETITION and are re-printed by permission of the Editor of the RADIO TIMES.

'One-pot' meals

Perhaps, like so many people nowadays, you have to cook on one gas-ring, a one-burner stove or an open fire. But there is no reason why you should put up with "scratch" meals. These real two-course meals for four people are planned to be well-balanced, delicious, and really practical. Here are seven suggestions:

MEALS without MEAT

Seven appetising meals without using the meat ration

ALL RECIPES FOR 4 PERSONS   ALL SPOONS LEVEL

FOODS TO USE INSTEAD OF MEAT

Meat is a body-building food and can be replaced only by one of the other body-building foods.

1. The best are : Milk (fresh, household or canned), Cheese, Fish (fresh or canned) and Eggs (fresh or dried).

2. Second best are : Soya flour, Dried Peas, Beans and Lentils, Oatmeal and Semolina.

Our bodies use a mixture of the two kinds very well.

M·F No. 29

Jam Making and Fruit Bottling

There is still a great shortage of food throughout Europe, and it is vital that everyone should help by growing all they can in gardens and allotments and preserving for winter use.

Home-made jams—" the sort that Mother makes "—and home-grown bottled fruits are the real thing : a source of pride to the housewife and of enjoyment to the family.

Preserve all you can : do not let any fruit be wasted. You will help yourself and help hungry Europe.

Making the most of the meat

Some people like to spread their meat ration over the whole week. Others prefer to use their ration for one good joint on Sunday. In this folder suggestions are made for both plans. For the first week, the meat ration is spread over five days, and off-the-ration dishes are suggested for the other two.

For the second week a roast is served for Sunday, and suggestions are made for off-the-ration dishes for the rest of the week.

D.2.

Defend the Kitchen Front!

A War-time Cookery DEMONSTRATION

will be held at

The C of E School

on

Monday, April 28th 2·30 p.m.

ADMISSION FREE

In co-operation with the HERTFORDSHIRE COUNTY COUNCIL

I pass this on to you

SOMETHING FOR TEA

By M. J. Mathieson

Miss Mathieson is the Secretary of the West Ham Branch of the Women's Gas Council, and a Home Service Adviser to the Gas Light & Coke Co. She took her training at the National Training College of Domestic Subjects and holds the Cordon Bleu for cookery.

MADEIRA CAKE WITHOUT SUGAR   CINNAMON BISCUITS
CANADIAN GINGER BREAD   OATMEAL BISCUITS
BAKEWELL TART   CHEESE SCONES
RASPBERRY BUNS   SYRUP SCONES
CHOCOLATE SANDWICH WITH ORANGE CREAM FILLING   DROP SCONES
ORANGE BISCUITS   OATMEAL SCONES

Series 8. No. 3

Potato Pete's recipe book

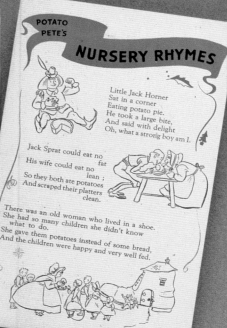

POTATO PETE'S
NURSERY RHYMES

Little Jack Horner
Sat in a corner
Eating potato pie.
He took a large bite,
And said with delight
Oh, what a strong boy am I.

Jack Sprat could eat no fat
His wife could eat no lean ;
So they both ate potatoes
And scraped their platters clean.

There was an old woman who lived in a shoe.
She had so many children she didn't know what to do.
She gave them potatoes instead of some bread,
And the children were happy and very well fed.

HELP TO WIN THE WAR... IN YOUR KITCHEN

NATURE DOES IT BEST

OFFER OF FREE COOKERY BOOK WITHIN

Try cooking Cabbage this way

LID TIGHTLY ON COOK FOR 10-15 MINUTES

CABBAGE SHREDDED COARSELY

JUST ENOUGH WATER TO COVER BOTTOM OF PAN

It's twice as delicious

PLEASE SEE ➔

DRIED EGGS

The Ministry of Food dried eggs are pure eggs with no addition, and nothing but the shell and the water taken away. They are pure eggs, spray dried. They are just as good as fresh eggs and can be used in the same ways. Here are some recipes for a variety of dishes, some of which can be used in place of meat, some in place of cheese.

TWO WAYS OF RECONSTITUTING DRIED EGGS

1 level tablespoon dried egg plus 2 tablespoons water equals 1 egg.

Either

Mix egg to a smooth paste with half the water. Beat till lumps have been removed. Add the remaining water and beat again with a fork or whisk.

Or

Mix the eggs and water and allow to stand for about five minutes until the powder has absorbed the water. This work out any lumps with a wooden spoon, finally beating with a fork or whisk.

USE AT ONCE

After reconstituting the eggs use at once. Do not reconstitute more eggs than necessary for immediate use.

HOW TO USE DRIED EGGS

Use in recipes exactly as fresh eggs, beating as usual before adding to other ingredients ; or for plain cakes and puddings, batters, etc., the eggs can be added dry and mixed with the other dry ingredients. When adding the liquid to the mixture an additional 2 tablespoons per dried egg used must be allowed ; or for cake and pudding mixtures where the creaming method of mixing is used, add the eggs dry, to the creamed fat and sugar. Beat well, gradually adding the amount of water required for reconstituting the eggs.

STORAGE

Keep the dried eggs in a tin with a tight fitting lid, and store in a cool place. Do not keep in a refrigerator.

MINISTRY OF FOOD — WAR COOKERY LEAFLET 11

Number 11

Dried Egg RECIPE SLIP   D.E.2

HOT BACON AND EGG SALAD (for 4 persons)

4 eggs, reconstituted
1 small cabbage
1 oz. flour
1 oz. margarine
½ pint vegetable liquid
1 teaspoon made mustard
Pepper and salt
Vinegar to taste
1 lb. new potatoes, cooked and sliced
2 or 3 carrots, cooked and sliced
½ lb. cooked peas
4 rashers bacon, cooked and chopped
1 onion or clove of garlic, grated

(Please turn over)

FUEL SAVING IN THE KITCHEN

Hedgerow Harvest

There is a wealth of wild foods in our hedgerows and fields for those who have within reach of the countryside. None of this should be wasted, but as there are always careful rules to be observed. There must be no broken fences, no gates left open for cattle to stray through, no trampling of growing crops or bushes or trees, no hurrying after fruit, no injury to the stalks of neatly pruned trees, no putting the roots of ... ... with a knife, leaving the roots intact.

Here are some recipes for using the hedgerow harvest. In the case of jams and jellies, it is important to remember that if they are required for keeping, the field should not be more than 2 lb. of preserve for each 1 lb. of sugar used.

MINISTRY OF FOOD LEAFLET No 5

Much effort was put into schemes for a better-fed nation under conditions of severe rationing. The people's health improved steadily as they ate turnip pie, haricot hot-pot and "war-and-peace pudding" (exotic names covered a multitude of commonplace ingredients).

Never before had there been such awareness of nutritional needs and the necessity for a balanced diet.

REVISED AND ENLARGED EDITION

WHAT TO EAT IN WARTIME

BY DUGALD SEMPLE

with MEATLESS RECIPES BY CATHIE SEMPLE

2/-

---

for 1 hour, covering with greaseproof paper when nicely browned.

SHEEP'S HEAD WITH CAPER SAUCE

4 TO 5 PERSONS

1 sheep's head	½ pint milk
2 pints water	1 tablespoonful capers
1 oz. flour	salt and pepper

Method.—Wash the sheep's head thoroughly in salt and water. Place in a pan and add the water. Simmer until tender—about 2 hours. Remove from pan and take out the tongue and the brains and cut the meat from the cheeks. Slice the tongue and the meat and put them with the brains on a dish and keep hot. Take ½ pint of the stock and ¼ pint milk and bring to the boil. Thicken with flour mixed to a paste with milk, and add the capers. Pour this sauce over the meat on the dish and serve.

The remaining stock and the sheep's head bones should be reboiled with the addition of vegetables and barley to make Scotch Broth.

VEGETABLE MARROW WITH LIVER STUFFING

4 TO 5 PERSONS

1 marrow	1 onion
½ lb. cold cooked liver	1 teaspoonful mixed herbs,
¼ lb. breadcrumbs	a little gravy, salt and
2 oz. suet or dripping	pepper

Method.—Peel the marrow, cut in half lengthways, scoop out the seeds. Mince the liver and the onion, add the breadcrumbs, herbs, suet, seasoning, and gravy and mix thoroughly. Stuff the marrow with this mixture and put the halves together. Tie up with tape, wrap in greased paper and bake until the marrow is tender. Serve with brown gravy made from bone stock.

DAILY EXPRESS WAR TIME COOKERY BOOK

1/-

FIRST FOODS TO BE RATIONED; EXTRA FOR INVALIDS

You MUST follow these rules for your ration book

Rations: The answers

Five foods will be rationed

4 oz. A WEEK IS FOR RATION

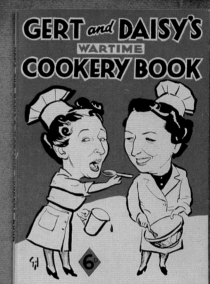

PENGUIN SPECIAL

F. W. P. CARTER

THE PENGUIN BOOK OF FOOD GROWING STORING AND COOKING

Seven suggestions for dinners which need no meat

· 1 ·
Pea vegetable and milk soup. Hard brown bread. Steamed fruit pudding.

· 2 ·
Eggs in savoury white sauce or savoury carrots. Greens. Potatoes. Apple charlotte or baked bread pudding.

· 3 ·
Potato, celery and milk soup. Curried beans and green vegetable.

· 4 ·
Stoved potatoes, oat cakes. Stewed apple pulp, dried or fresh, and cornflour. Glass of milk.

· 5 ·
Fresh or tinned fish, potato, beetroot and cress salad. Milk pudding and jam or sultanas.

· 6 ·
Parsnip, carrot and potato pie, gravy, greens. Bottled plum pulp and custard. Glass of milk.

· 7 ·
Artichoke and potato milk soup. Beetroot, cress, bean and carrot salad with sweetened dressing.

National Wheatmeal bread to be served with each meal.

RATION DINNERS

Homely Savoury Dishes adapted to war conditions for Families & Canteens

2D

Published by THE CENTRAL COUNCIL FOR HEALTH EDUCATION TAVISTOCK HOUSE, TAVISTOCK SQUARE, LONDON, W.C.1

WARTIME FOOD FOR *Growing* CHILDREN

From the Ministry of Food's KITCHEN FRONT BROADCASTS

FOURPENCE NET.

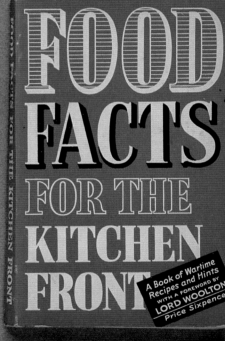

GERT and DAISY'S WARTIME COOKERY BOOK

6d

The Stork Wartime Cookery Book

THE KITCHEN FRONT

NATIONAL ROLY-POLY

CRUST	MEAT, ETC.
6 oz. National flour	6 oz. cooked mixed vegetables
1 oz. suet	5 ozs. cooked beans
1 oz. grated raw potato	4 ozs. minced beef
1 teaspoonful baking powder	
Pinch of salt	
Water to mix	

For Crust :
Rub the fat into the flour, add the baking powder, salt and grated raw potato. Mix to a stiff dough with cold water (it might take a little more water than usual). Roll out and your dough is ready.

For Filling :
Cream all filling ingredients together, spread on your rolled-out dough, roll up as usual and either steam it for an hour and a half, or bake it in a moderate oven for 40 minutes to 1 hour. If you are steaming, wrap the pudding in a floured cloth. If you are baking, roll it in oatmeal. You will find the oatmeal will toast a most succulent brown.

RABBIT STEW WITH PRUNE DUMPLINGS

1 rabbit	1 tablespoonful dripping
1 bay leaf	2 tablespoonfuls flour
2—3 large carrots	Salt and pepper. Water.

FOR THE DUMPLINGS :
8 cooked prunes (they should not be too soft)
6 ozs. flour ½ oz. lard or cooking fat
½ teaspoonful salt

Put the jointed rabbit and the carrots, sliced, into a saucepan with the bay leaf and a seasoning of salt and pepper. Cover with water and bring to the boil. Remove all scum, then simmer gently for 1 hour. Strain off ½ pint of the liquor. Melt the dripping, add the flour and blend thoroughly. Stir in the boiling hot liquid to make a smooth thickened sauce. Put back the rabbit and the carrots.

To make the dumplings, rub the fat into the flour and salt, moisten with enough cold water to make a soft dough. Roll out and divide into 8 pieces. Wrap a stoned prune in each piece. Mould into 8 dumplings, drop into fast boiling salted water and cook quickly 8—10 minutes. Skim them up and put them in with the rabbit and carrot. Serve at once.

12

The KITCHEN FRONT

122 WARTIME RECIPES broadcast by Frederick Grisewood, Mabel Constanduros and others, specially selected by the Ministry of Food.

6D. NET

FOOD FACTS FOR THE KITCHEN FRONT

FOOD FACTS FOR THE KITCHEN FRONT

A Book of Wartime Recipes and Hints WITH A FOREWORD BY LORD WOOLTON Price Sixpence

---

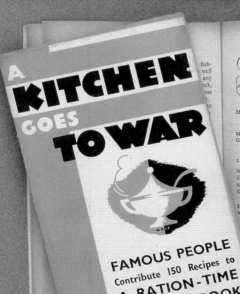

A KITCHEN GOES TO WAR

FAMOUS PEOPLE Contribute 150 Recipes to A RATION-TIME COOKERY BOOK

Meat and Poultry

MOSTLY UNRATIONED

M. GABRIEL VALLET, Maitre Chef de Cuisine, Grosvenor House.

BRAINS FRITTO

2 sets calves' brains.

METHOD: Cook the brains in salted water, adding a drop of vinegar. Allow to cool, then cut in pieces and dip in batter. Fry in smoking hot fat or oil, drain well and serve with tomato sauce.

HELEN SIMPSON says her dish requires a good heart.

CABBAGE STUFFED WITH SAUSAGE MEAT

METHOD : Take a fresh cabbage with, as far as you can feel, a good heart. Cut away the outer leaves. Take a pointed knife with a serrated blade and cut into pieces.

Mr. Arthur Webb, on page 108, tells how to make batter.

35

GOOD HOUSEKEEPING BOOK OF **Thrifty War-Time Recipes**

Economical Vegetable, Fish, Meat & Game Dishes

Soups and Salads

Approved by the MINISTRY OF FOOD

6D

• A 100 WARTIME CHEESE RECIPES •

A HUNDRED CHEESE RECIPES

By Ivan Baker

The Housewife's help in the use of her cheese ration

Ninepence

• A 100 WARTIME CHEESE RECIPES •

TO YOUR THOUGHTS SEND HIM A
TMAS CARD

SAFEGUARD YOUR FRIENDSHIP SEND CHRISTMAS CARDS

Coupons for Butter Coupons for Cheese Coupons are needed for these and these and Coupons for most that we want and see But "WISHES" thank goodness are Coupon Free VERY MANY GOOD WISHES FOR YOUR BIRTHDAY

May you have BAGS of GOOD LUCK and no SAND in your eye this CHRISTMAS

Will you be my Valentine —and my King of Hearts.

It may be from Tommy

It may be from Jack

Or from the Boy in Air Force Blue

Will you be my Valentine —and my Queen of Hearts

"GOT NO COUPONS !!.... but—plenty of Birthday Wishes for you!"

for VALENTINE and VICTORY

Christmas Greetings FROM THE CIVIL DEFENCE
POLICE
WARDENS
RESCUE PARTY AND DEMOLITION
STRETCHER PARTY
AMBULANCE
FIREMEN

I'LL BE YOUR WALTZING MATILDA IF YOU'LL BE MY VALENTINE?

CHRISTMAS GREETINGS 1944
NEW YEAR GREETINGS 1945
Send him GREETINGS on a CHRISTMAS AIRGRAPH form

TMAS CARDS ALL AT HOME

The morale of the fighting services suffered if they did not receive regular mail from home. Greetings cards were readily adapted to the mood of the moment, and valentines had the service men and women in mind.

23

BESTWAY FASHIONS Nº 234

War-time RENOVATIONS
8d

Free Patterns for both FROCKS and COATS inside

Renovation Ideas for Children's Clothes Included

Leach-Way FASHIONS Nº 147

ECONOMY FROCKS
Average & Small Sizes
7d

These 3 Patterns FREE Inside

6d Home Front FASHIONS
(WOMEN, CHILDREN & MEN)

★ WITH SMART FINISHING TOUCHES VIA YOUR SEWING MACHINE

SINGER

40 Smart Styles for NOW with charming accessories

VOUCHER FOR PAPER PATTERN (Value 6d.) FREE

FREE PAPER PATTERN! (VALUE 6d) *Choose any design inside.* SEE PAGES 1 & 16

BESTWAY FASHIONS Nº 236

COATS and SUITS from Short Lengths
8

SUIT takes 2⅜ yds 11 COUPONS

COAT takes 2⅜ yds. 11 COUPONS

SAVE ON STOCKINGS
Silktona

LIQUID SILK STOCKINGS

Gives bare legs the Elegance of Sheer Silk

SUFFICIENT FOR 24 APPLICATIONS

PERI-LU STRAND DARNING Special FINE ART. E.65

With clothes coupons restricting the number of new purchases, making your own or, at least, mending your own clothes became part of everyday life. Sachets or bottles of "liquid silk stockings" could be bought, or gravy browning was an adequate substitute.

WELDON KNITTING SERIES No. 24

6ᵈ

NEW WOOLLIES for our SAILORS, SOLDIERS and AIRMEN

Instructions for 20 COMFORT Designs

MEND AND MAKE-DO TO SAVE BUYING NEW

MAKE-DO AND MEND

MAKE DO AND MEND LEAFLET No. 7

PATCHES

Patches are **important**—every one you put on helps you to put off buying something new. And it's just as easy to patch properly as to cobble. Half the battle is knowing how to cut and place your material...

CHART LEAFLET No. 3 ISSUED BY THE BOARD OF TRADE

HOW TO PATCH ELBOWS AND TROUSERS
by Mrs. SEW-and-SEW

CHART LEAFLET No. 4 ISSUED BY THE BOARD OF TRADE

HOW TO PATCH SHEETS AND BLANKETS
by Mrs. Sew - and - Sew

PERI-LUSTA STRANDED DARNING

Knitting for the R.A.F.

OFFICIAL BOOK OF INSTRUCTIONS

1/-

ROYAL AIR FORCE Comforts Committee
20 Berkeley Sq. LONDON. W.I.

HINTS ON WASHING

MAKE DO AND MEND

WHERE'S THAT MOTH?

UNPICK AND KNIT AGAIN

DECORATIVE PATCHES

PREPARED FOR THE BOARD OF TRADE BY THE MINISTRY OF INFORMATION

Price 3ᵈ net

PERI-LUSTA STRANDED DARNING

Specially prepared for FINE SILK HOSE

MAKE DO AND MEND
COATS CLARK

CHART LEAFLET No. 1 ISSUED BY THE BOARD OF TRADE

HOW TO PATCH A SHIRT
by Mrs. SEW-and-SEW

● Shirts are easy to mend, as the patches can be cut from other parts of the garment. They can be replaced by similar material cut from a discarded shirt, or soft cotton. When the cuffs start to fray, they should be carefully unpicked and reversed. As they are double, the worn edge will then be inside the fold. If you are using new fabric for patching...

Economy Design SIZE 32. No. 1

25

Punch 1/-

What The Empire Women Are Doing—

READ THEIR LETT ON PAGE 8

Weekly **WELCOME** 2291 FEB 24 1940 PRICE 2ᵈ

AND **WOMAN'S WAY**

A Real Comfort for Tommy

KNIT THIS WARM PULLOVER FOR YOUR MAN ON ACTIVE SERVICE

everybody's 2ᴰ

RUG-MAKING FOR BLACK-OUT NIGHTS

WOMAN'S FRIEND 2ᵈ

Home Notes 3ᵈ ON SALE SATURDAY, AUGUST 19, 1944

ILLUSTRATED 3ᵈ

PROGRAMMES FOR July 19—25

PRICE TWOPENCE

RADIO TIMES

JOURNAL OF THE BRITISH BROADCASTING CORPORATION

(INCORPORATING WORLD-RADIO)

"TripleX" — the safety glass

1/6

THE SPHERE

WITH WHICH IS INCORPORATED THE GRAPHIC OCTOBER 25 1941

Brilliant Story by Christine Jope-Slade

Woman's Own

3ᴰ Every Friday Aug 24.1940

GOOD TASTE JULY 1943 NINEPENCE

PICTURE POST

THREEPENCE

Woman EVERY THURSDAY

FREE complete stories by NORAH RYOTT • ROBERT CARSON SHIRLEY DARBYSHIRE

Make your Jam with our help

Most magazines were published throughout the war, but contained fewer pages. Patriotic covers abounded, but many continued with their pre-war format. "Jane's Journal" featured the popular "strip" queen of the "Daily Mirror" (since 1931) always accompanied by her dog Fritz.

What's Your War Work? SEE ARTICLE INSIDE

HOME NOTES 3ᵈ

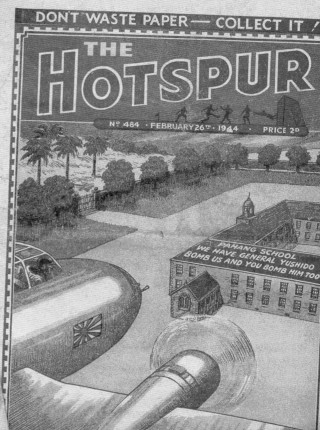

Comics for younger children did not dwell on the war, but for older children the glamorous side of battle was there in all its glory. By the end of 1942 the size of "Meccano Magazine" and "Boy's Own Paper" had been halved to save paper. Doubtless the

28 stories of heroes and articles like "Are you fit for flying?" made youngsters look forward to active service.

BOY'S OWN PAPER

JANUARY, 1942

No. 472. Vol. 19

GIRLS' CRYSTAL
and "THE SCHOOLGIRL"
Week Ending Nov. 4th, 1944. 3ᵈ

ALONE AGAINST THE INVADERS

A Girl's War-time Adventures On A Lonely Pacific Island Are Featured In This Thrilling Complete Story—By AUDREY NICHOLLS.

WHEN DANGER THREATENED

"DARANEE, you dream too many dreams and think too many thoughts," Madge Bryant smiled kindly. "Of course the Japs will never come to the Isle of Orchids. What next will you and your...

STORIES OF POWER-AND PEP-AND PUNCH!

A bunch of the best in the best of the bunch!

ADVENTURE
EVERY MONDAY 2ᵈ

NO. 996
NOV. 30TH
1940

FOLKS WITH FADS!

The Magnet
THE MAGNET THRILLING DETECTIVE-ADVENTURE YARN OF GREYFRIARS! 2ᵈ

THE CHAMPION
and TRIUMPH
MEET COLWYN DANE, DETECTIVE, INSIDE
No. 1,172. Vol. 46. Every Friday. Week Ending July 15, 1944. 3ᵈ

LEADER OF THE LOST COMMANDOS

AIR STORIES
WAR-FLYING FICTION OF TO-DAY 7ᵈ

APRIL

TRIUMPH
"TRIUMPH 2ᵈ Every Tuesday" LOOK! ORDER TRIUMPH DOUBLE-LENGTH STORY of MAD CAREW Inside

MECCANO MAGAZINE
VOL. XXIX. No. 9 SEPTEMBER 1944

AFTER THE TEST FLIGHT 6ᵈ

RADIO FUN
MEET YOUR RADIO STARS FLANAGAN & ALLEN • WILL FYFFE • SANDY POWELL • ARTHUR ASKEY • REVNELL & WEST and OTHERS INSIDE! 2ᵈ
"BIG-HEARTED ARTHUR" No. 34. June 3rd.

BOY'S OWN PAPER

A scene from "THE SECRET OF ROSMERSTRAND" (beginning inside)

APRIL 1942 9ᵈ IN CANADA 20 CENTS

THE ROVER
"BRITAIN'S SECRET WEAPON" ATTACKED FROM THE AIR!
No. 936—MAR. 16th, 1940. EVERY THURSDAY 2ᵈ

THE WIZARD
LOOK OUT FOR NEWS OF MORE
No. 1042 JAN. 22, 1944 PRICE 2ᵈ

29

Toy manufacturers devised war-related games to wile away the long black-out evenings. Jig-saws depicted the latest military skirmish and war leaders, and if throwing darts at Hitler's face became boring, you could "decorate Goering" by closing your eyes and pinning medals on his chest, in the same way as "Pinning the tail on the Donkey".

The Battle of the River Plate in December 1939 created the opportunity for one enterprising firm to devise "The Greatest Naval Game ever known". A wooden ship could be fired at with a torpedo, scoring points according to where it hit; a direct hit released the turrets.

She's in Love with a Soldier

DAVID HENEKER
& NOEL GAY

"Potato Pete"

by SONNY MILLER and HUGH CHARLES

HI-HI!
BUY-BUY!

HEN CAN I HAVE A BANANA AGAIN?

WORDS & MUSIC BY
NAT MILLS
GABY ROGERS
& HARRY ROY

BLUE LABEL
FYFFES
BRAND
BANANAS

The Morris
MUSIC PUBLISHING CO LTD
1 NORRIS ST
HAYMARKET
LONDON SW1

ROLAND'S PIANOFORTE TUTOR · THE BEST IN THE WORLD
ENGLISH FINGERING   CONTINENTAL FINGERING
Nº 3061.   Feldman's 6ᵈ Edition

TILL THE LIGHTS OF LONDON SHINE AGAIN

SONG FOX-TROT

UKULELE GUITAR
PIANO-ACCORD

"GOOD LUCK—

and the same
to you!"

I shall be waiting

Words & Music by
ROSS PARKER
HUGHIE CHARLES
and JOE IRWIN

FEATURED & BROADCAST BY
SYD LIPTON
AND HIS GROSVENOR HOUSE DANCE BAND

A sing-song in the air raid shelter kept morale up and continued the pre-war tradition of community singing. Topical songs included "When can I have a banana again" (1943): "I get along without sugar. I never drink any tea, eggs and bacon, beef and ham, these things don't worry me ... but one thing I always crave, and that's why you hear me sing, 'Oh! ....." etc.

LET'S GO -

WINGS FOR VICTORY

W.F.P. 270. ISSUED BY THE NATIONAL SAVINGS COMMITTEE, LONDON, THE SCOTTISH SAVINGS COMMITTEE, EDINBURGH, AND THE ULSTER SAVINGS COMMITTEE, BELFAST.

PRINTED FOR H.M. STATIONERY OFFICE BY HAYCOCK PRESS, LONDON. 51-3074

Spot them in the Air!

PUBLISHED BY THE
DAILY MIRROR
3D

I is for

16.

J is for

a
JITTERY
JUNKERS. 87.

THIS IS A GERMAN DIVE BOMBER known to everybody as the Stuka. Its ugly features include fixed undercarriage and heavy jowl-like radiator. Its crew of two sit in ... and with a siren seeks ...

A.B.C. of
AEROPLANE
SPOTTING

by Haynes

A
TUCK
BOOK

COPYRIGHT   PRINTED IN ENGLAND

RAPHAEL TUCK & SONS LTD
Fine Art Publishers to T.M. the King & Queen & to H.M. Queen Mary.

U is for

a
THOR'S
THUNDERBOLT.

an
UNUSUAL
HURRICANE.

THIS LARGE AMERICAN SINGLE SEAT FIGHTER is noted for its high flying qualities. Its 2,000 h.p. Double Wasp motor gives it a top speed of 400 m.p.h. and it is armed with eight heavy machine guns. Recognized by a blunt nose, a wing shaped like a section of an orange and a heavy tapering fuselage, the Thunderbolt is the biggest fighter of its class.

ELDER BROTHER OF THE TYPHOON, this fighter is most versatile. The Mark II series have a 1,280 h.p. Merlin motor and are armed with 12 machine guns or 4 cannons. The tank buster has two heavy cannons slung under the wing. Capable of carrying a 1,000 lb. bomb load the Hurricane has a humped back, equal tapered wings and a large rounded fin and rudder.

SPOT THEM IN THE AIR!
Published by the "Daily Mirror"

GERMAN & ITALIAN
AIRCRAFT
HOW TO SPOT THEM
THE ONLY COMPLETE ILLUSTRATED RECORD

281st Thousand

1/3 NET

A UNIQUE COLLECTION OF PHOTOGRAPHS,
SILHOUETTES & ILLUSTRATIONS, WITH
EXPLANATORY NOTES DEPICTING ALL TYPES
OF GERMAN AND ITALIAN AIRCRAFT

A PENGUIN SPECIAL
R. A. SAVILLE-SNEATH'S
Second book of
AIRCRAFT
RECOGNITION

A PENGUIN SPECIAL
R. A. Saville-Sneath
AIRCRAFT
RECOGNITION
(REVISED)

VOLUME I REVISED

SPOT THEM AT SEA!

BRITISH & GERMAN
TROOP
CARRIERS
and
SEAPLANES
BRITISH
TRAINERS

British
and
German
FIGHTERS
AND
BOMBERS

AIRCRAFT
IDENTIFICATION
FRIEND OR FOE?

PREPARED BY
The AEROPLANE

PART TWO
(REVISED)

TEMPLE PRESS LTD.

AIRCRAFT
IDENTIFICATION
FRIEND OR FOE?

PREPARED BY
The AEROPLANE

PART ONE
(REVISED)

TEMPLE PRESS LTD.

Part One
2/-
Revised

Aircraft identification was an essential part of war — for those in the street it was something akin to train spotting.

Grow for Winter as well as Summer

DIG FOR VICTORY

THIS PLAN WILL GIVE YOU YOUR OWN VEGETABLES ALL THE YEAR ROUND

HOW TO DIG

DIG FOR VICTORY LEAFLET NUMBER 20 (NEW SERIES)

ISSUED BY THE MINISTRY OF AGRICULTURE

DIG FOR VICTORY

For their sake—
GROW YOUR OWN VEGETABLES

Radio Times, June 5, 1942. Vol. 75. No. 975. Registered at the G.P.O. as a Newspaper

PRICE TWOPENCE

RADIO TIMES

JOURNAL OF THE BRITISH BROADCASTING CORPORATION

(INCORPORATING WORLD-RADIO)

PROGRAMMES FOR June 7—13

This Week

THE RADIO ALLOTMENT

In this London garden twenty-three different types of vegetables are being grown, as well as a large variety of herbs. Once a week its progress is broadcast to gardeners all over the country.

SPRING and SUMMER will come as usual—
EVEN in WARTIME

DO NOT BLACK-OUT YOUR GARDEN
OR YOU MAY REGRET IT LATER

Plant now:

Hyacinths, Daffodils, Tulips, Crocus, Polyanthus, Wallflowers, Perennials, Fruit Trees, Roses, Hardy Trees & Shrubs

(NO RATIONING)

EXPERT ADVICE

SPRING WARTIME GARDENING GUIDE
WHAT TO GROW AND HOW TO GROW IT

1/6

Issued in support of THE MINISTRY OF AGRICULTURE'S "DIG FOR VICTORY" CAMPAIGN

by P. DYER, N.D.H., D.I.P.A.
Edited by ROY HAY (of B.B.C. "Radio Allotment")

A VICTORY LIBRARY BOOK — SERIES 1 NUMBER 1

ALL GARDENERS

MUST COME AND SEE A NEW COLOUR FILM ENTITLED

"A Garden goes to War"

WHICH WILL BE SHEWN AT

The Memorial Hall, Chorley Wood

ON

Wednesday, Feb. 19th, at 6.45 p.m.

THE FILM WILL BE FOLLOWED BY A TALK ON LOCAL GARDENING PROBLEMS

BY

MR. A. C. BAIRD

ADMISSION FREE

COME AN...

IS YOUR GARDEN ON WAR SERVICE?

EVERYTHING FOR YOUR GARDEN at..

Timothy Whites and Taylors
HOUSEHOLD STORES

178-180 HIGH STREET, SUTTON.

Telephone Vigilant 1896.

BRANCHES THROUGHOUT GREAT BRITAIN.

GROW MORE FOOD

DIG FOR VICTORY

CROWN COPYRIGHT RESERVED

Your own vegetables all the year round...

if you

DIG FOR VICTORY NOW

Cuthbert's Famous Seeds

GROW MORE FOOD

RADISH CUTHBERT'S EXHIBITION FRENCH BREAKFAST

3D.

BEET
EARLY CRIMSON GLOBE

For earliest sowings sow on a warm border in February or March in drills ½ inch deep in rows 12 inches apart, or later for succession.

Quittenden's SEED ESTABLISHMENT

ESTABLISHED 1799 — HAWKHURST, KENT

Happy Hours on the Food Front

TUCK BOOK

Gardeners were encouraged to dig for victory, with help for beginners by way of booklets like "How to dig" and films entitled "A Garden goes to War". The children's booklet "Happy Hours on the Food Front" describes how Daddy (in the Home Guard, of course) enjoys working in the garden growing vegetables. The last page is captioned "There are plenty of vegetables in the market - thanks to all the people who have worked hard growing them in their fields and gardens."

DIG FOR VICTORY

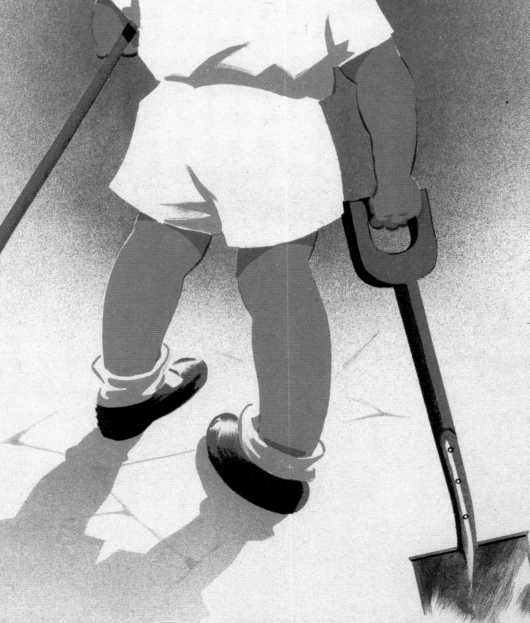

The nation's sweet tooth had to contend with the rationing of confectionery from July 1942. An allocation of points to everyone restricted sweet consumption to 3oz per head per week. Wrappers and cards indicated the controlled price and category into which a product fell. The lack of full-cream milk meant that separated milk was used, the result being termed "blended chocolate". The familiar red of the Kit Kat

wrapper turned to blue indicating that it was now plain chocolate. Many wrappers were eventually made from grease-proof paper and advertising display cards were in short supply, shopkeepers hanging on to pre-war examples. Newspaper advert: inside an air raid shelter "Got your gas mask? Got your Bassetts?"

For a healthy, happy job

Join the
WOMEN'S
LAND
ARMY

CLIVE UPTTON

for details:
APPLY TO NEAREST W.L.A. COUNTY OFFICE OR TO W.L.A. HEADQUARTERS 6 CHESHAM ~~PLACE~~ LONDON S.W.1 STREET

Issued by the Ministry of Agriculture and the Ministry of Labour and National Service

PP 130

PRINTED FOR H.M. STATIONERY OFFICE BY W. R. ROYLE & SON LTD.—51-2989

40

Come on the Services!

LEND A HAND ON THE LAND

SPEND YOUR LEAVE OR SPARE TIME

HELPING FARMERS

FULL DETAILS

Week ending June 24 1944   THREEPENCE

Woman

EVERY THURSDAY

Help to Pick.... Help to Store

Woman's Own

3D.
Every
Friday
Sep.14,1940

DO YOU DO IT THIS WAY? - Sewing Secrets Inside

MY HOME

9d
SEPT. 1941

Crochet YOURSELF These COSY SLIPPERS

WOMAN and HOME

AND GOOD NEEDLEWORK Magazine

9d
MAY
1942

Rug Wool Slippers

THE **LAND** GIRL

No. 3, Volume 3   JUNE, 1942   Price 3d.

ADAPTABILITY

THE **LAND** GIRL

No. 8, Volume 4   NOVEMBER, 1942   Price 3d.

GOOD NIGHT(S), LADIES

LIFE IN THE
LAND ARMY

Hearty cheers for the boys at the
front and for the Land Girls
behind as well!

The Women's Land Army worked on farms all over
the country to bring in the harvest, sow the seed,
tend the cattle, and pick the fruit. A letter to "The
Land Girl" concludes "after putting in the regulation
50 hours plus overtime during the harvest, we have
cropped our garden of half an acre, I have a green
house full of tomatoes, and have made about
50 lbs of jam and some pickles."

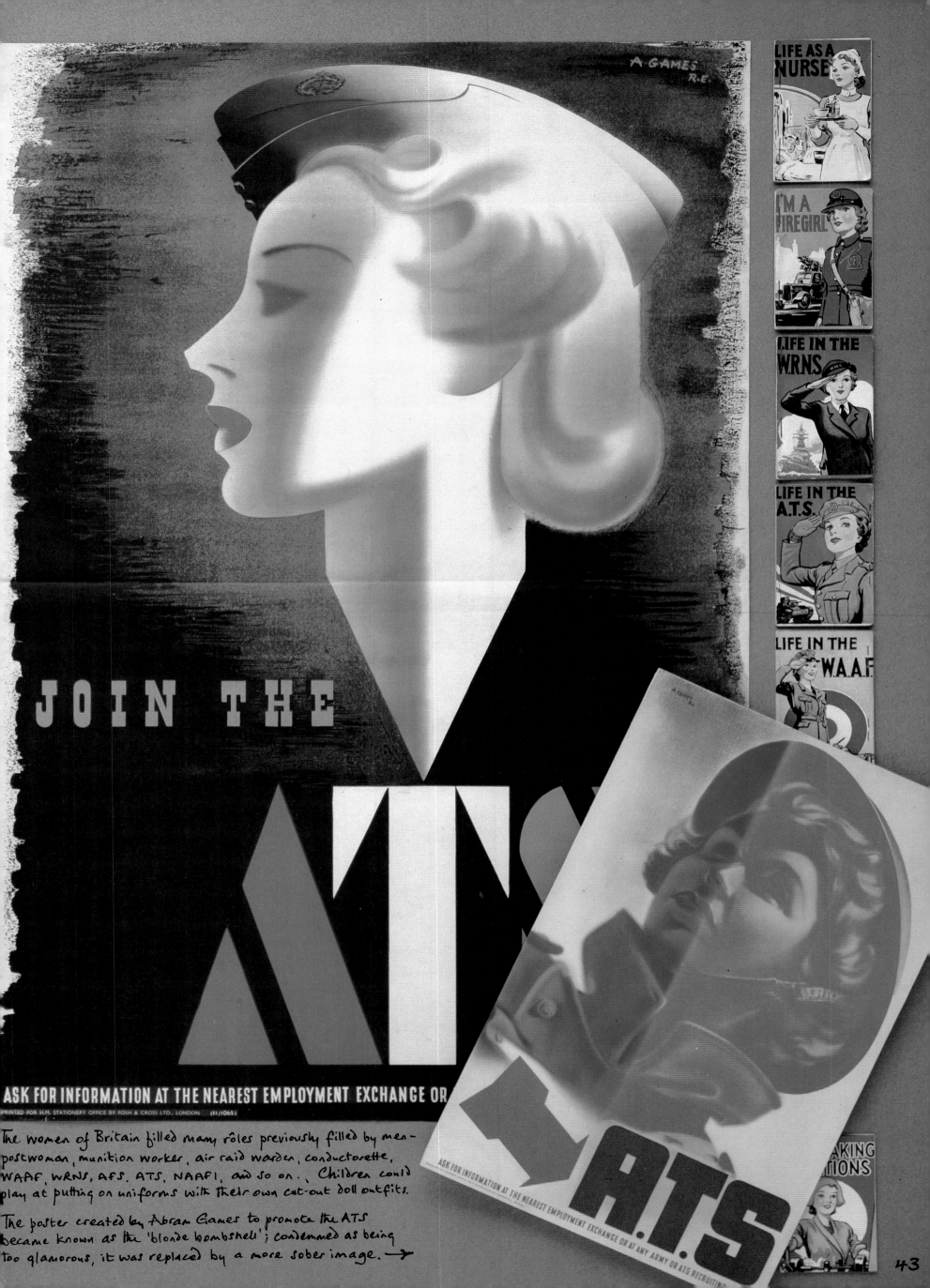

JOIN THE

ATS

ASK FOR INFORMATION AT THE NEAREST EMPLOYMENT EXCHANGE OR

PRINTED FOR H.M. STATIONERY OFFICE BY FOSH & CROSS LTD., LONDON.   (51/1065)

A. GAMES
R.E.

LIFE AS A NURSE

I'M A FIREGIRL

LIFE IN THE W.R.N.S.

LIFE IN THE A.T.S.

LIFE IN THE W.A.A.F.

A.T.S

ASK FOR INFORMATION AT THE NEAREST EMPLOYMENT EXCHANGE OR AT ANY ARMY OR ATS RECRUITING

The women of Britain filled many rôles previously filled by men –
postwoman, munition worker, air raid warden, conductorette,
WAAF, WRNS, AFS, ATS, NAAFI, and so on., Children could
play at putting on uniforms with their own cut-out doll outfits.

The poster created by Abram Games to promote the ATS
became known as the 'blonde bombshell'; condemned as being
too glamorous, it was replaced by a more sober image. →

everybody's

2D

R.A.F.'S TWENTY-FIFTH BIRTHDAY
(page 8)

SPECIAL WAR-TIME CATALOGUE OF
FREE GIFTS
SOMETHING FOR EVERYBODY

HORNIMAN'S TEA
FAMOUS SINCE 1826
ALL PRE-WAR LISTS CANCELLED - 1940

laughs with the
Forces
1/3

"IT'S A PIECE OF CAKE!"

R.A.F SLANG MADE EASY
BY
S/Ldr. C.H. WARD-JACKSON
with drawings by
DAVID LANGDON

R·A·Fing it
by
"L.A.C ERRANT"
SKETCHES BY EDGAR NORFIELD
FREDERICK MULLER LTD
LONDON
1/- net

Taking Off!
by
NOEL MONKS
ILLUSTRATED WITH AUTHENTIC PHOTOGRAPHS

A TUCK BOOK

Service men have a natural instinct to create their own jargon — "bubble dancing" meant washing up one's plates. Cartoonists reflected the legendary resilience of the fighting man, or not ... Captain, "Any deficiencies?" Private, "Never bin issued wiv any, Sir." The Home Guard started their parade from May 1940. The butt of many jokes, they themselves took the task seriously ... and so did their manuals.

HOME GUARD

Humour

1/6

THE NAVY'S HERE!

FRANK·H·MASON, R.I.

DRILL

UP-TO-DATE

A Short Manual for the HOME GUARD

PRICE **6** D. NET

Close Order Drill at the Halt
Close Order Drill on the Move
Platoon Drill
Company Drill
Battalion Drill
Arms Drill

FOR FREEDOM!

A PANORAMIC PICTURE STORY BOOK OF OUR

NAVY · ARMY & AIR FORCE

The HOME GUARD POCKET MANUAL

Price 6d.
No. 192
Revised Edition

Xmas 1942. With... Much love
& good wishes from... Annie

Our RAILWAYS in War-time

THE HOME GUARD.

"There'll always be an England,"
And no enemy can rob
A Briton of his freedom
While the Home Guard's on the job!
Peer and page and ploughman,
You're on patrol to-day
For England, home, and beauty!
And mean to do your duty
In the good old British way ;
The one-time Sergeant-Major,
Captain, and Colonel too—
You're proud to serve as privates now,
So here's good luck to you!

a full-blown Private now!

We should worry!

Laugh It Off

Make way there for the lorry
That goes hurtling down the road,
With warning bell that rings to tell
The nature of its load!
And at the sound the folk around
All stop and turn and stare
To see the heroes flashing by—
But do the heroes care?
They sit at ease, they cross their knees,
They chat and smile and nod—
It's just the daily round, you see,
To the bomb disposal squad!

When lengthy is the butcher's queue,
And joints and sausages are few,
We say, while facing fearful odds,
"It's on the knees of all the gods
What we shall have for dinner!"
Try as we will, we can't foresee
What portion of what beast 'twill be
Of which we'll be the winner.
Some animals now seem to grow
About a hundred tails or so,

While others have no
Perhaps we'll be cont
A kidney or a bit of t
Or dine off [rationed]
But if at last away we
Our coupons' worth o
What joy the proud h
Triumphant, home we
And set it forth to wo
Peace-time had no suc

Tin-hatted Muse ! thy Respirator doff !
Emerge from Shelter, now the Raid is off !
Salute the glad Return of Christmas-tide,
Tho' Huns have spread their Havock far & wide.
Shall frantick Hitler, or his paunchy Aide,
Or twisted Goebbels shed a gloomy Shade ?
No ! Let them rage, in Night Tartarean sunk,
Goaded by Ley & waited on by Funk.
Bare we our Fangs in better Cause—to sup—
And, like the Christmas-tree, be all lit up ;
Sweet Victory, th' appointed End, is near ;
Meanwhile, " A happy Christmas & New Year "

Little drops of water, little grains of sand,
Lots and lots of buckets standing close at hand,
Yards and yards of hose-pipe ready in the hall—
That's the stuff to give 'em when incendiaries fall!

Like a blinkin' firework show, whizz and bang and pop!
Everybody's watching to see the blighters drop;
Every Jane and Susan, every Dick and Tom
Is running to extinguish an incendiary bomb!

The British sense of humour helped win the war —
keeping up morale and smoothing the propaganda
machine. In any crisis there was always someone
who could laugh it off. A Birmingham wine
shop owner announced across his bombed
premises, "We are carrying on with unbroken
spirits"; a London pub proclaimed, "Blown
out, blasted out, but not sold out."

en Tommy has a song to sing,
t's not of fame and glory,
tle, wounds, or anything
That's bellicose and gory—
es a love-song, one that tells
A moving human story!
f it should be over-long,
His voice not over sweet,
find the boys regard his noise
As if it were a treat,
e's as good a fellow
As you'd ever wish to meet!

alling me.

swipe

ps or steak,
lls!
the prize
ng eyes—
lls!

REGISTER HERE

GET THERE ON A .....

GAZELLE

THE GAZELLE NOTTINGHAM ENGLAND

WARNING UNEXPLODED BOMB

DROP IN FOR A CATALOGUE

PRINTED IN ENGLAND

Bang and flare and crackle, what a beastly glare!
What a smell of bonfires filling all the air!
Boys and girls and grandmas, with an eager shout,
Quickly fall upon them, and soon each one is out!

Wouldn't the Luftwaffe throw a bloomin' fit
If they saw the cheery way Britons GO TO IT?

WHEN on CIVIL DEFENCE DUTY
you are one of two things—
either inside or out on a job.
If you are inside you need not worry.
If you are out on a job you are one of two things—
either in a danger zone or not.
If you are in a danger zone which is not dangerous
you need not worry.
If you are in a danger zone which is dangerous
you are one of two things—either wounded or not.
If you are slightly wounded you need not worry.
If you are seriously wounded one thing is certain—
either you will get well or not.
If you get well you need not worry.
If you die you cannot worry.
Therefore you need not care a damn!

AMBULANCE

FIRST AID POST

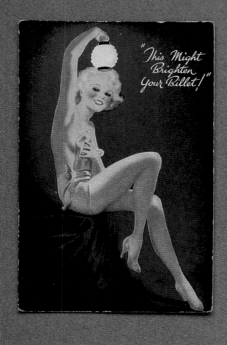

"This Might Brighten Your Billet!"

"'ERE, CAN'T YOU READ?"

Though they ration petrol, tea or meat
I swear by Heaven above,

They never will or can control
That sloppy thing called 'Love'!

WHEN CAN WE "MEAT" AGAIN?

WHO WANTS BLINKING SEARCHLIGHTS TO-NIGHT?

A "BAMFORTH" COMIC

"He grabbed my ration-book, Officer, and tried to pinch my Personal Points!"

"A blow on the Siegfried line!"

"You an' your go to bed early to save coal an' light!!"

"WE HAD AN ESCAPED GERMAN PRISONER HIDING IN OUR HOUSE LAST NIGHT!"
"HOW DID YOU KNOW?"
"I HEARD MUM TELL DAD THERE WAS A JERRY UNDER THE BED!"

I GOT HER WITH A PARCEL OF SOLDIERS' COMFORTS, SIR!

A "BAMFORTH" COMIC

"HAVE THESE CHILDREN BEEN EVACUATED?"
"NOT YET SIR—I'M JUST MIXING THEM UP A DOSE!"

CHILDRENS WELFARE

IT'S ALL BECAUSE OF HITLER
YOUR SUGAR RATION'S LITTLER!
IT'S ALL BECAUSE OF HITLER
THE COST OF MILD AND BITTER!
IT'S ALL BECAUSE OF HITLER
THE PETROL RATION'S HIT YER!
BUT REMEMBER THIS, MY FRIEND,
WHEN AT NIGHT YOU
GROPE ABOUT,
ADOLF'S GOING TO PAY FOR THIS---
HIS LIGHT WILL BE PUT OUT!

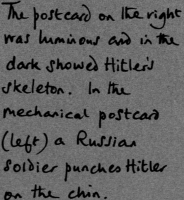

NOW—CAN I COVER MY TOES—OR BLOW MY NOSE?

"This Might" "This Front is quite Active!"

PULL   GLORIOUS STALINGRAD.

The comic postcard provided a good laugh as well as a convenient form of communication. All the pre-war illustrators, especially Donald McGill and Mabel Lucie Attwell, were on hand to create their miniature masterpieces.

The postcard on the right was luminous and in the dark showed Hitler's skeleton. In the mechanical postcard (left) a Russian soldier punches Hitler on the chin.

This man of troth once wrote a book And called the tripe "Mein Kampf", But now we know he mashed it wrong, It should have been "Mein Ramp!"

To see the doom of this Nazi spark Hold this card to the light and look in the dark.

"Are we good? I ask you, how the blazes could we be otherwise in all this clobber?"

LOOK AT THAT, YOU FOOL---AND YOU MADE AN AIR RAID WARDEN THIS MORNING!

A "BAMFORTH" COMIC

Maid: "The siren's gone. Missus says you've to go in the dug-out!"
Lodger: "I won't, the cistern's not working!"

YOUR UNITS MUST NOT BE DISCLOSED!

CENSORED

"I wish to offer you my apologies, Gentlemen,--- I have sometimes referred to the Nazis as Swine!"

"I WISH I'D COME HERE BEFORE THE WAR!"
"NICE OF YOU TO SAY THAT, SIR!"
"NICE MI EYE! THIS BLUE PENCIL EGG MIGHT HAVE BEEN FRESH THEN!"

A "BAMFORTH" COMIC

JOLLY UNSPORTSMANLIKE I CALL IT!

"WAS THAT A BOMB?"
"NO,—IT WAS ONLY ME."

"WOOL WITHOUT COUPONS!"

CARELESS TALK MAY GIVE AWAY VITAL SECRETS

KEEP IT DARK—
I'LL BE SEEING YOU SOON!

DON'T LET SUCH THINGS WORRY YOU---

THINGS ARE NEVER AS BAD AS THEY SEEM!
WHY THE "DEUCE" NEED WE WORRY IF WE PLAY THE GAME, OLD BEAN!

I'M TELLING YOU!

N.B.G. COMMERCIAL TRAVELLER

IF HITLER WANTS ANY MORE TERRITORY
HE CAN HAVE MINE!

GOSH! I WISH I'D ONE O' THEM DICTATORS HERE---
JUST FOR TWO MINUTES!

IT WON'T BE ALL SMOOTH GOING—WE'LL JUST HAVE TO GO CAUTIOUSLY FOR A TIME!

A "BAMFORTH" COMIC

"Lummy, if I got 'old of him, I'd tear 'is Swastika off!"
"My! Ain't you bloodthirsty!"

"There's two chaps I'd like to give a kick in the pants. Hitler an' that ruddy Quarter bloke!"
"Why, what's Hitler done?"

WITH THE HOME GUARD

"ADVANCE FRIEND AND BE RECOGNISED"

PHOTOCHROM COPYRIGHT.   HOME GUARD SILHOUETTES. No. 3

The Americans arrived in January 1942 bringing vital new energy and generous supplies of cigarettes, chocolate, chewing gum and nylon stockings.... a few envious British voices could be heard to mutter, "What's wrong with the GI's? They're over-fed, over-sexed, and over here!"

MINISTRY OF LABOUR
MUNITION CONCERTS

ORGANISED BY
E.N.S.A.

Keep THIS Flag flying!

JUNE 8th 1943

NATIONAL FLAG DAY
for the RED CROSS & St JOHN

The PLANE road to BERLIN

METROPOLITAN
BOROUGH OF
FULHAM
WINGS FOR VICTORY
MARCH 6   WEEK   MARCH 13

WAR WEAPONS WEEK
APRIL 12-19
£100,000
to be saved
during the week
RICKMANSWORTH AND
CHORLEYWOOD DISTRICTS.

STALINGRAD WEEK—MALVERN, 1943
(Registered under the War Charities Act. 1940.)
"BOBS" for BEDS
IN THE NEW HOSPITAL IN STALINGRAD

HOUSE TO HOUSE
COLLECTIONS ACT
Mrs. CHURCHILL'S
RED CROSS
"AID TO RUSSIA"
FUND

Help the Spitfire-Fund

SPITFIRE FUND
& EMPIRE PROPAGANDA STAMPS

An important part of raising funds, especially
for the smaller causes (as in the First World War)
was the flag day - appeals for everything from
the National Air Raid Distress fund to District
Nursing Flag Day. The traditional steel pin was
eventually replaced by a button hole tab, examples
of which can be seen here →
Every week had its allocated appeal from
War Weapons Week to Stalingrad Week.

RED CROSS & S^T JOHN

 *needs your help*

SEND YOUR GIFT TO ST. JAMES'S PALACE, LONDON, S.W.I

THIS APPEAL IS BEING MADE BY THE DUKE OF GLOUCESTER'S RED CROSS AND ST. JOHN FUND, ST. JAMES'S PALACE, S.W.I, ON BEHALF OF THE WAR ORGANISATION OF THE BRITISH RED CROSS SOCIETY AND THE ORDER OF ST. JOHN OF JERUSALEM. REGISTERED UNDER THE WAR CHARITIES ACT, 1940

A well stocked larder! Most brands survived, some were replaced, like Stork margarine with National margarine.
Breakfast cereals were 'zoned' so that only one variety was obtainable in a certain part of the country.
Most packs eventually put on their "war-time jackets" (see Orlox Suet top shelf centre), which meant using poorer

quality cardboard, reducing the size of the label, replacing tin with card and using less printing ink. Consumers were urged to save cartons for salvage; for each Oxydol pack saved two cartridge wads could be made, thus "Two more nails in Hitler's coffin". Mazawattee Tea and Ridgways ARP Tea pointed out that their tins were "gas proof" being hermetically sealed.

DAILY EXPRESS

No. 14,012   Coast dim-out 9.55 pm to 6 am   WEDNESDAY MAY 2 1945   Moon rises 2.36 am (Thurs) sets 10.30 am   One Penny

GERMANS PUT OUT THE NEWS EVERYONE HOPES IS TRUE
Drum-roll heroics—then the build-up of hero-leader fighting to his last breath

'HITLER IS DEAD'

Doenitz goes on radio:
I am your new Fuhrer

OBITUARY

THE Daily Express rejoices to announce the report of Adolf Hitler's death. It prints today every line of information

It gives no picture of the world's most hated face.

It records that Hitler was

Victory night—

I SMELL PINEAPPLE

Daily Mail

VICTORY EDITION

NO. 15,290   ONE PENNY ★ ★ ★ FOR KING AND EMPIRE   TUESDAY, MAY 8. 1945

TUESday FIELD-DAY

3 POWERS WILL ANNOUNCE GREAT SURRENDER SIMULTANEOUSLY

VE-DAY—IT'S ALL OVER

The King to speak to Empire: Victorious generals will follow Premier on radio

Joy-day throngs stop traffic

IN NEW YORK

From Daily Mail Correspondent
New York, Monday.

NEW YORK went wild with excitement when the first unofficial victory report was received. Within a few minutes more than a million people were out in the streets celebrating.

VICTORY ISSUE
May 8, 1945

News Chronicle

No. 30,881   TUESDAY, MAY 8 1945   ONE PENNY

TODAY IS V DAY

Churchill speaks at 3 p.m., the King at 9; Today and tomorrow are national holidays

TODAY IS V DAY, MORROW IS PUBLIC HOLIDAY. THIS WAS FOLLOWING OF

"It is understood in accordance with arrangements between the three Great official announcement broadcast by the Prime three o'clock tomorrow May 8.

"In view of this fact Tuesday, will be treated in Europe Day and garded as a holiday following, May 9, holiday.

"His Majesty the broadcast to the pe British Empire and Co tomorrow at 9 p.m.

"Parliament will usual time tomorrow

THANKSGIV

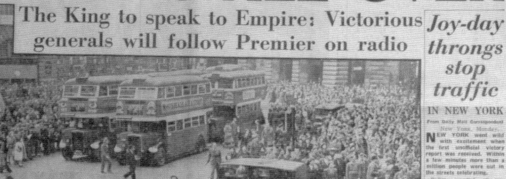

VICTORY SOUVENIR CARD

PRESENTED BY
R. DOWNS & CO.
WITH COMPTS
RETAIL
STATIONERS
71, Lytham Road
BLACKPOOL

VICTORY
CUT-OUT BOOK

DEAN

26

Peace at last and lots of spontaneous celebrations. Every available mug was quickly pressed into service as a victory souvenir. More prestidgious victory items were available, cut-out books and scarves, but few in number owing to the scarcity of raw materials.

V F-OR VICTORY

FOR
THE PERFORMANCE
OF
TASK ALLOTTED

has shewn a high sense of Duty and Discipline and has made a valuable contribution to the War Effort of the Country for Final Victory over the Enemy

ISSUED BY THE
MINISTER OF SUPPLY

WELCOME BACK

Victory

Daily Mirror
FORWARD WITH THE PEOPLE
ONE PENNY

PEACE
JAPAN SURRENDERS—
ALLIES CEASE FIRE

Piccadilly, caught napping, woke up

Today and tomorrow V-days "Enjoy yourselves" call by Attlee at midnight

"PEACE HAS ONCE AGAIN COME TO THE WORLD. LET US THANK GOD FOR THIS GREAT DELIVERANCE AND HIS MERCIES." IT WAS THE VOICE OF THE PRIME

Answer to a Riddle

RADIO TIMES
2ᵈ

BBC
Victory Programmes

THURSDAY, MAY 10,
to FRIDAY, MAY 18, inclusive

National Thanksgiving Service
from St. Paul's Cathedral

Mr Churchill broadcasts on Thursday
and Mr. Eden on Sunday

Their Finest Hour—In honour of
the Royal Navy, the Army, the R.A.F.,
the Merchant Navy, and the People
of Britain

Victory Music-Hall and The Stars
Come Out with star Variety
artists

Will Hay celebrates at St. Michael's

The Kentucky Minstrels

Jack Buchanan and Elsie Randolph
in Stand Up and Sing

J. B. Priestley on Journey
into Daylight

Celebrations from all parts of the
United Kingdom

Conan Doyle's The Adventure of
the Speckled Band

Special Programmes for the Children

COOKERY SERVICE
NOTES No. 70
NOVEMBER, 1945

HOME FRONT
COOKERY ADVICE

VICTORY CHRISTMAS

GRAND PICTORIAL
SOUVENIR

THEY LED US
TO VICTORY

DIEU·ET·MON·DROIT

Official Programme
of the
VICTORY
CELEBRATIONS
8th June
1946

8th June, 1946

TO-DAY, AS WE CELEBRATE VICTORY,
I send this personal message to you and
all other boys and girls at school. For
you have shared in the hardships and
dangers of a total war and you have
shared no less in the triumph of the
Allied Nations.

I know you will always feel proud to
belong to a country which was capable
of such supreme effort; proud, too, of
parents and elder brothers and sisters
who by their courage, endurance and
enterprise brought victory. May these
qualities be yours as you grow up and
join in the common effort to establish
among the nations of the world unity
and peace.

George R I

VICTORY CORD
THREE YARDS
ONE YARD OF EACH — RED,
WHITE AND BLUE
USE FOR TRIMMINGS OR TO
FOLD YOUR OWN VICTORY
FAVOURS   9ᵈ PER 1YD (INC. P TAX)

G R
1939   1945

V. E Day

MAY. 8th. 1945

VE
VJ

Here's a space for your own
FAMILY MEMORIES

The war of words — informing, persuading, cajoling, encouraging. These posters employed the great commercial artists of the day including Bateman, Gilroy, Games, Giles, Casson, Purvis, Mount, Lewit-Him, Zéro, Fougasse.

"Beat the Blitz" (1941). This pea canner had fun during this board game, so try it out — its great fun (you will need a spinner or dice plus some counters). Follow the progress of Benedict English Peas — a race against air raids and time bombs, road jams and tank traps, warnings and diversions!

41
42
43

40

44
45 BACK To 39. To AVOID MANOEUVRES
46
UNEXPLODED TIME BOMB BACK To 46. TAKE SIDE RD. 47
48

43

39

42

41

48
49

DANGER

50
NAZI PLANE ON VIEW ADMISSION 3° "SPITFIRE"

CLEAR ROAD.
38
DOUBLE LAST THROW

BOMB CRATER. BACK TO No 36 AND USE SIDE RD.

40

POLICE TO MOVE TO

39
SIGNALS PASS TO 41

51 DRIVER STOPS NEAR THROW '2' TO GET AWAY

52

LAND FOR SALE

38

51

37

TANK-TRAP
37
THROW A '4' TO GET OUT.

SPORTS-GROUND

52

53

36

FLOODS

54

35

55 DRIVE SLOWLY. MISS A THROW.

34

56

PARK

33

57

32

BENEDICT WORKS

58

61

62

31 MAN LORRY MISS A THROW

59

60 BACK TO No 38. LORRY COMMANDEERED BY MILITARY.

GATE-CHECKS LOAD A

30

29

28

PLAYERS HERE FOR 27 MUST LAND PACKING.

TESTING FOR 26 VITAMIN CONTENT.

CANN- 25 -ING.

GRADING. 24 FAIL TO PASS GRADE GO RIGHT BACK TO No 1.

CLEANSING 23 PROCESS.

PODDING 22 SHELLING.

BENEDICT ENGLISH PEAS.

21

WAIT FOR 20 UNLOADING. MISS A THROW.

19

18

17

TAKE FURTHER SUPPLIES. 16 MISS A THROW.

15

14

13

THROW EXACT No TO LAND

BENEDICT

YEOVIL COLLEGE LIBRARY

DESIGNED & DRAWN BY JADE' 1940